NATIONAL GEOGRAPHIC

My Walk

Zoe Sharp

T0052117

SUBURBAN
S
ATHLETICS

2 Bell Court

DE EAST
OL 4386
130

OPEN 7 DAYS
HOME DELIVERY
SUBURBAN
ATHLETICS

SUPERMARKET
ideal dairy
SUPERMARKET
ATM
cash
Available Here
ATM
cash
Available Here
Streets
International Roast
$5.00
Weekly Special
$1.00
Weekly Special
Weekly Special
Potting Mix

SILVER SPOONS
COFFEE
PASTRIES
CAKES
Eat in or Takeaway
SUBURBAN
S
ATHLETICS

POONS

Gifts
for
Better Homes and Gardens
FREE GOLD STARS
CHRISTMAS!

Photos
SUBURBAN
S
ATHLETICS

Animal
Hospital
IVANHOE
SURGEON

15

SUBURBAN
S
ATHLETICS